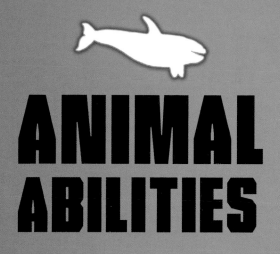

ANIMAL ABILITIES

ORCAS

Anna Claybourne

Chicago, Illinois

© 2013 Raintree
an imprint of Capstone Global Library, LLC
Chicago, Illinois

To contact Capstone Global Library, please
call 800-747-4992, or visit our web site
www.capstonepub.com

Edited by Laura Knowles, Abby Colich,
    and Diyan Leake
Designed by Victoria Allen
Original illustrations © Capstone Global
    Library Ltd 2013
Illustrated by HL Studios
Picture research by Elizabeth Alexander
Originated by Capstone Global Library Ltd
Printed and bound in China by CTPS

17 16 15 14 13
10 9 8 7 6 5 4 3 2 1

Library of Congress Cataloging-in-Publication Data
Claybourne, Anna.
  Orcas. -- (Animal abilities)
Cataloging-in-Publication data is available at the
Library of Congress.

ISBN (PB): 978 1 4109 5246 2
ISBN (HB): 978 1 4109 5239 4

Acknowledgments
We would like to thank the following for
permission to reproduce photographs: Alamy
pp. 6 (© Accent Alaska.com), 17 (© Mark Boulton),
20 (© Nic Hamilton), 22 (© Alaska Stock), 24
(© Brandon Cole Marine Photography); Corbis
pp. 9 (© Tory Kallman/National Geographic
Society), 13 (© Ralph Lee Hopkins/National
Geographic Society), 15 (© Hiroya Minakuchi/
Minden Pictures), 21 (© Theo Allofs); © Innespace
Productions, Inc./www.seabreacher.com p. 27;
naturepl pp. 5 (© Brandon Cole), 18 (© Kathryn
Jeffs), 25 (© Bryan and Cherry Alexander);
Photoshot pp. 7 (AllCanadaPhotos), 8 (NHPA/
Gerard Lacz), 29 (Maxi); Press Association Images
p. 11 (Phelan M. Ebenhack/AP); Shutterstock
pp. 4 (© Tom Middleton), 16 (© CampCrazy
Photography), 19 (© Irina Silvestrova), 23 (© Glen
Gaffney), 28 (© bikeriderlondon), orca silhouette
on various pages (© Thumbelina).

Cover photograph of an orca reproduced with
permission of FLPA (Gerard Lacz).

Every effort has been made to contact copyright
holders of material reproduced in this book.
Any omissions will be rectified in subsequent
printings if notice is given to the publisher.

Contents

Some words are shown in bold, **like this**. You can find out what they mean by looking in the glossary.

Meet the Orca

Orcas are big, muscular sea **mammals** with giant **dorsal fins** and bold, black and white markings. They are easy to tell apart from other sea creatures.

What is an orca?

Orcas are also called killer whales, but they are actually a **species** (type) of huge **dolphin**. A male weighs around 7 tons and can reach 33 feet (10 meters) long—around the size of a bus! His dorsal fin alone can be as tall as a fully grown man.

Orcas are mainly black, with white undersides and eye patches.

Orca abilities

Orcas can do some amazing things. They leap high out of the water, detect food using echoes, and play with toys. They work as part of a team, learn to do tricks, and seem to be able to "talk" to each other. Like some other whales and dolphins, they are thought to be very intelligent.

Orcas will leap out of the sea and splash back down. This is called breaching.

ARE THEY KILLERS?

Orcas are meat-eaters and powerful **predators**. They can hunt in groups to catch **prey** bigger than themselves. They were called "whale killers" because they sometimes hunt whales, and this name later became "killer whales." But don't worry — they are hardly ever dangerous to humans.

Being an Orca

Although orcas only breathe air, they spend their whole lives in the sea. They are diurnal, which means they are mostly active during the day. They spend most of their time traveling, hunting, resting, or just playing.

This group of orcas is on the move off the coast of North America.

On the prowl

Orcas spend a lot of time looking for food. If they are eating fish, they may spend half their time hunting. If they are chasing large mammals such as seals, it may take them almost all day. That is because large mammals are harder to find and catch, and take longer to eat.

Half asleep

Like other whales and dolphins, orcas can't fall asleep completely, or they would not be able to come to the surface to breathe. Instead, one half of an orca's brain falls asleep, while the other half stays awake. Orcas can take naps at any time, but they usually spend a lot of the night snoozing.

ARE ORCAS ENDANGERED?

Orcas are not **endangered**. However, they are at risk from threats such as fishing and pollution.

These fishermen may be waiting for orcas to leave the area. Orcas will often steal fishermen's catch.

Orca Bodies

Orcas are air-breathing mammals, like humans. Although they live in the sea, they cannot breathe underwater. But their bodies are very well **adapted**, or suited, to a watery lifestyle.

Orcas swim so strongly that their whole body may lift out of the water.

FAST FLUKES!

Orcas can zoom through the water at a top speed of more than 30 miles (around 50 kilometers) per hour.

Built for the sea

Orcas breathe through their **blowholes**. Blowholes are a bit like our nostrils, but they are positioned on top of the orca's head so that it can breathe easily while swimming. Orcas also have a **streamlined** shape and thick, smooth skin to help them slide quickly through the water.

In this picture, you can see all of an orca's main body parts.

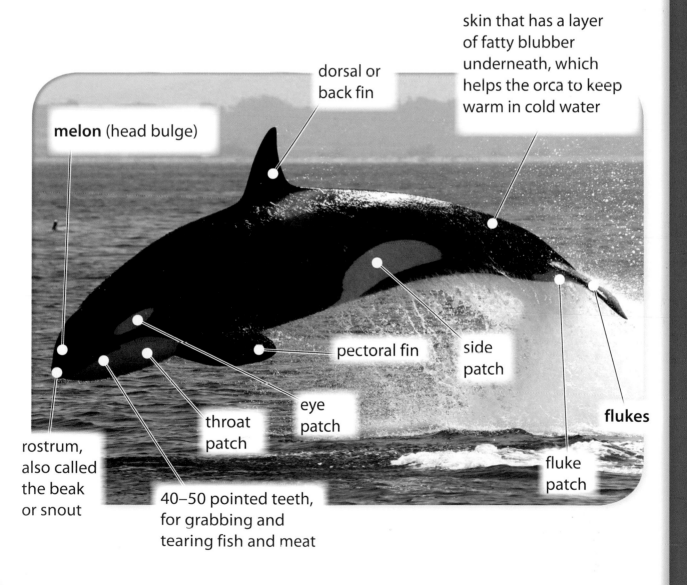

melon (head bulge)

dorsal or back fin

skin that has a layer of fatty blubber underneath, which helps the orca to keep warm in cold water

pectoral fin

side patch

flukes

eye patch

throat patch

rostrum, also called the beak or snout

40–50 pointed teeth, for grabbing and tearing fish and meat

fluke patch

Orca Brains

Bigger animals usually have bigger brains, while smaller animals have smaller ones. But an orca's brain is about 2.5 times as big as you would expect for its size—a sign of high intelligence.

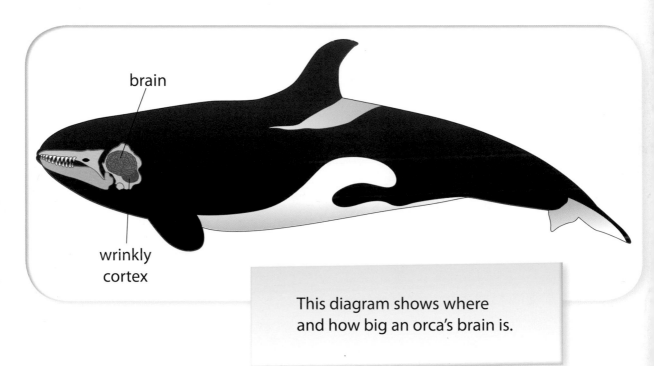

brain

wrinkly cortex

This diagram shows where and how big an orca's brain is.

Brains for thinking

When scientists looked closely at orcas' brains, they found that they are not only big, but also very wrinkly, like human brains. This means that orcas have a large cortex, which is the outer layer of the brain used for thinking and memory. To fit around the brain, the big cortex has to fold and crinkle. Orcas have special brain cells called spindle cells, which are also found in humans and some other intelligent animals. Spindle cells are thought to be used for emotions, love, and caring.

These **captive** orcas are learning to follow instructions from their trainers.

HOW DO WE KNOW?

When most animals look in a mirror, they just see another animal. But in tests with mirrors, orcas seem to be among the few animals that realize they are seeing themselves. This may show a "sense of self"— another feature of intelligent creatures.

Orca Senses

Orcas' most important sense by far is their amazing hearing. They communicate using noises and also use sound to detect and catch prey.

Echo vision

Orcas have good eyesight, but their hearing gives them an even better way of "seeing," called **echolocation**. To use it, an orca sends out a beam of clicking noises that bounce off underwater objects, such as rocks, fish, or seals. The orca senses the echoes and uses them to build up a "picture" in its brain. Orcas can recognize different types of fish with echolocation, even in darkness.

Orca echolocation

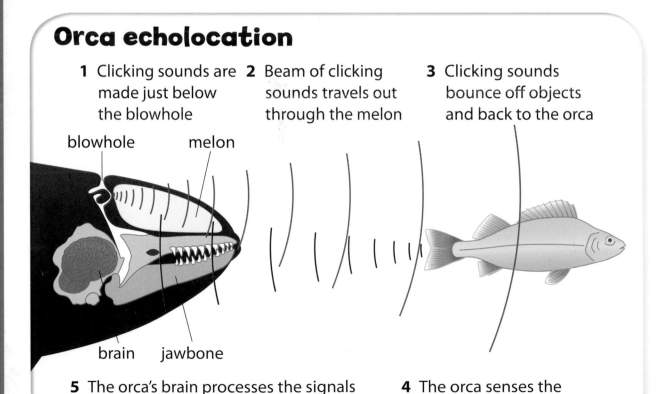

1 Clicking sounds are made just below the blowhole

2 Beam of clicking sounds travels out through the melon

3 Clicking sounds bounce off objects and back to the orca

blowhole   melon

brain   jawbone

5 The orca's brain processes the signals to work out what the object is

4 The orca senses the echoes using its jawbone

Sensitive skin

Orcas have a very good sense of touch, too. They love to nuzzle, nudge, stroke, and scratch each other as a way of being friendly. The skin around an orca's blowhole is especially sensitive to **water pressure**, so the orca can tell when it is about to break the water surface and can take a breath.

As its blowhole clears the surface, an orca breathes out fast.

HEAR THIS!

Orcas have earholes, but they do not use them much for hearing. Instead, sound vibrations travel through an orca's head and jawbone to the hearing parts of the ear inside its head.

Orca Groups

Many orcas live in small family groups called **matrilines**. Each one is led by an orca mother. Even as adults, orcas can stay with their mother for as long as she is alive. Some young orcas go off and join other matrilines.

Orca matriline

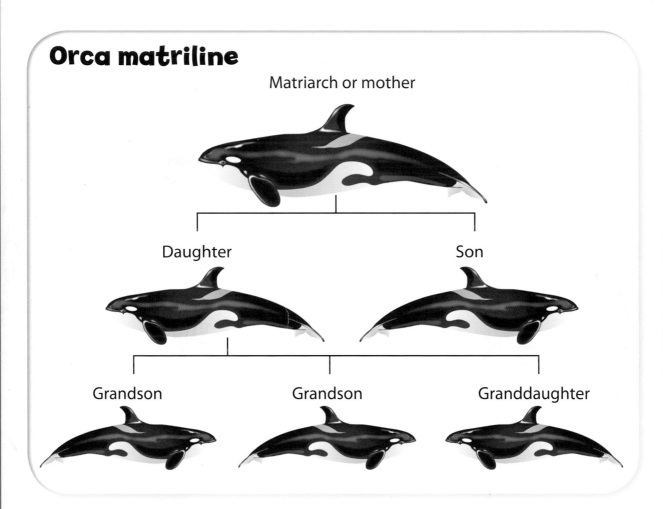

Matriarch or mother

Daughter

Son

Grandson

Grandson

Granddaughter

Pods and clans

A **pod** is a larger group of orcas, made up of several related matrilines. Pods of around 50 orcas often travel and feed together. Even bigger groups, called **clans**, are made up of all the related orcas in the area.

Meeting and mating

Every few years, a female orca finds a mate from outside her own pod and has a baby, or calf. After mating, males and females do not stay together—they return to their own matrilines. When the calf is born, it feeds on thick, fatty milk from its mother's body.

Orca calves constantly touch and nuzzle up to their mothers.

HOW DO WE KNOW?

We actually do not know much about how orcas find a mate, since it is hard to spot this happening in the wild. Scientists think they may get together in extra-large mating groups so that males and females can meet up. We can also learn about mating by seeing the behavior of captive orcas in aquariums.

Orca Talk

Orcas are very good at communicating with each other. They make sounds by taking air in through their blowhole. However, the sound does not come out of the blowhole. Instead, the orca sends it through its melon. This fatty organ in its forehead seems to let it direct sound wherever it wants to.

An orca beams out sounds using its melon.

Orca speech

Orcas can make many different sounds. They include echolocation clicks, long whistles, and a range of high-pitched squeaks, moans, trills, and grunts. Scientists do not understand all these calls, but some experts think they could contain complex messages. Orcas can hear each other over long distances, since sound travels well through water.

Orca "accents"

Scientists have found that each orca pod has its own "**dialect**"—a particular pattern and style of sounds, like human accents. This helps orcas to keep track of their own pod and also to spot orcas from other pods.

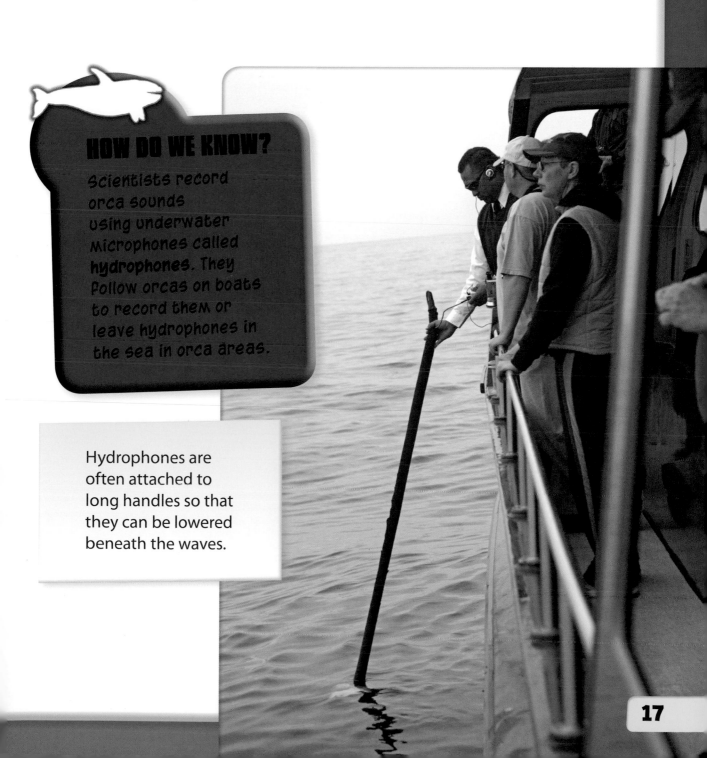

HOW DO WE KNOW?

Scientists record orca sounds using underwater microphones called **hydrophones**. They follow orcas on boats to record them or leave hydrophones in the sea in orca areas.

Hydrophones are often attached to long handles so that they can be lowered beneath the waves.

Learning and Training

Some orca abilities, such as echolocation, are **instincts**. They come naturally and do not have to be learned. However, orcas are also good at learning new things and have good memories.

Look at this!

Orcas seem to be able to invent new ways to do things, and then they learn from each other. For example, in 1979, a small group of orcas was first seen making waves to knock seals off an **ice floe**. At the time, it was thought to be a one-time event. Since then, it has become much more common, as other orcas have picked up the ability and passed it on.

These orcas are checking out their prey before trying to knock it into the water.

Captive orcas perform tricks at aquarium shows.

Performing orcas

Orcas can also be trained to do tricks. There are aquariums where captive orcas perform shows in a huge pool, doing amazing leaps and balancing acts. Some have even learned to let trainers ride them!

IS IT RIGHT?

Many people think orcas should not be held in captivity, partly because they are so large and need space, and also because they naturally form large groups. But trainers often say their captive orcas are happy, and scientists can also learn a lot from them. Who do you think is right?

Growing Up

Like human children, orcas grow up slowly. They take around 10 years to reach adulthood and can live for more than 50 years. As orca calves grow up, they learn a lot from their mothers and from the others in their matriline and pod.

Learning a language

Young orcas have to learn to "talk" using the dialect of their own pod (see page 17). They also learn to tell the difference between their own pod dialect and other dialects. Scientists have found that orca dialects can change gradually over time—just as human languages and accents change over the years. Orcas copy and learn these changes from each other, so they get passed down through generations.

Like human babies, orca calves learn by watching and copying adults.

Do it like this!

Orcas have been seen carefully teaching hunting methods to their calves. For example, orcas in some areas have developed a hunting method that involves lunging up onto the beach to grab seals. Orca mothers have been seen pushing their calves ashore toward the seals, to show them how to do it.

This male orca is using the beach-surfing hunting method to catch its prey.

Having Fun

Many animals appear to enjoy playing. It is likely that this is part of the way they hunt and feed. Orcas also show the need to behave in this way. Otherwise, they may get bored. This is one of the arguments against keeping them in captivity.

Orcas appear to communicate with each other when they splash in the sea.

Playing in the wild

Wild orcas often play with each other. They chase and leap after each other, nudge and poke each other gently, and roll and splash around. They will also chase after boats for fun and ride on the waves they make. Orcas sometimes play with kelp seaweed, dragging it along with their fins and tails. They have also been seen throwing and catching dead seals before eating them.

People are fascinated by orcas wherever they can see them.

Watching me, watching you

Some orcas live in zoo-type aquariums, where they do not perform tricks, but have visitors who come to watch them. They sometimes seem to play games with people through the glass, copying what they do or making dancing movements. They are also given toys to keep them busy, such as balls, tires, and mirrors.

STORY TIME

Some aquarium orcas even seem to enjoy looking at books about orcas!

Humans and Orcas

Humans have been fascinated by orcas since ancient times. The Roman writer Pliny the Elder described the orca as "an enormous mass of flesh armed with savage teeth"!

This rock carving of an orca in Washington state was made 300 years ago.

Orca beliefs

Some American Indian peoples believed orcas could change into human form and lived in houses under the waves. Others thought they were the kings of the sea. One ancient American Indian model of an orca dates from 4,000 years ago, and orcas are often found carved onto totem poles and canoes.

The age of whaling

In the past, humans hunted whales and dolphins for their meat and blubber. Orcas were not a main target because they are fast and hard to catch. But when supplies of bigger whales ran low, whalers caught thousands of orcas—until most whaling was banned in the 1980s. Some orcas still die in fishing nets or are killed by fishermen who want to protect their own catch.

ARE ORCAS DANGEROUS?

Wild orcas are usually described as friendly and inquisitive when they meet humans and do not attack swimmers or divers. However, orcas in captivity have sometimes attacked and killed their trainers.

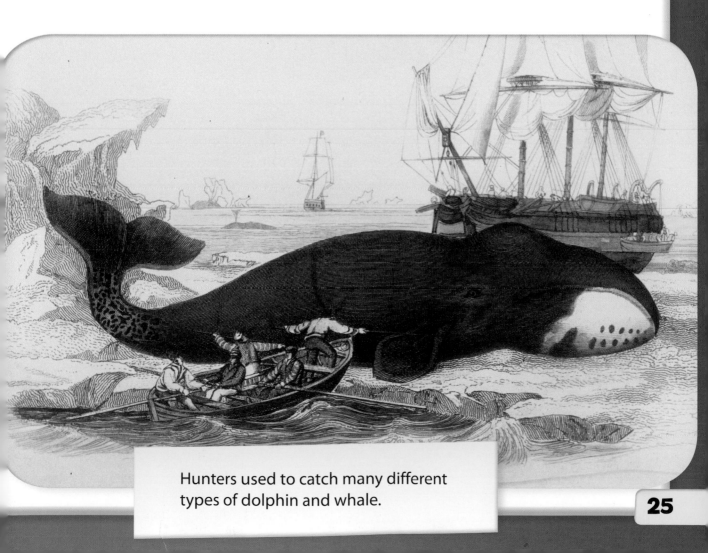

Hunters used to catch many different types of dolphin and whale.

Copying Orcas

Since orcas can do quite a few things we cannot do, they have inspired us to build new creations and inventions that are based on their amazing abilities or that work in a similar way.

Sonar systems

Sonar is a way of using echoes to "see" underwater. It works like the echolocation found in orcas and other whales and dolphins as well as in bats, which use echolocation in the air. We use sonar to map the seabed, search for sea creatures, or locate deep-sea submarines.

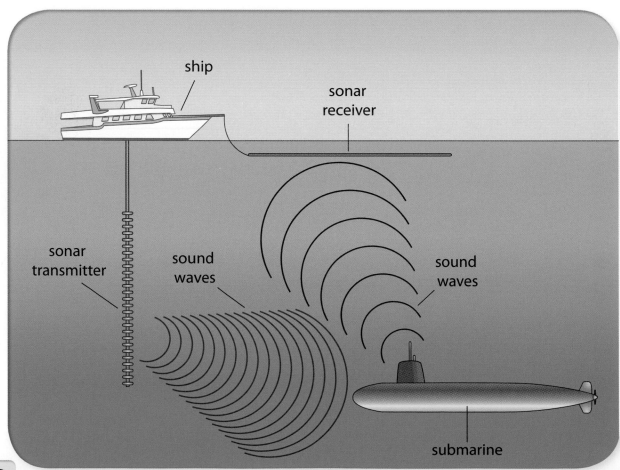

ship

sonar receiver

sonar transmitter

sound waves

sound waves

submarine

Listen like an orca

Hydrophones often don't work in deep water, as water pressure pushes on their delicate sensors. Orcas don't have this problem. They can make the pressure inside their ears match the water pressure outside. One inventor copied orca ears and invented a hydrophone with tiny holes in it that let water through. The water pressure is equal inside and outside, and the sensors are not crushed.

ORCA SUBMARINE

One boat-building company has made an orca-inspired watercraft called Seabreacher Y. It is shaped and painted to look like an orca, and it can dive, leap, and splash like the real thing, with the driver riding inside.

The Amazing Orca

Though we once saw orcas as simply big, fierce sea creatures, we now know that they are much more than that. Their sensing, swimming, and hunting abilities are amazing, and then on top of that, they are super-smart. In fact, some scientists who work with them think they could be the most intelligent animals of all.

Orcas can swim five times faster than humans.

Orca superpowers

If you could borrow one of the orca's superhuman abilities, what would it be?

- Super-strong tail: You would break every swimming record in the world with the orca's tail. You would zoom along at up to 30 miles (about 50 kilometers) per hour, and you could do thrilling leaps—although you might want to make your tail detachable.

- Echolocation: Even with your eyes closed, you could sense where objects were as well as their shape and movements. This would be very useful for blind people.

- Superhuman hearing: You could have a conversation with your mom from your friend's house without a phone! Or you could stick your head into the sea and listen to all the sea creatures communicating.

Some people who have lost their sight develop basic echolocation abilities—but not as good as an orca's.

Glossary

adapted   developed to suit the environment

blowhole   breathing hole in the top of a whale or dolphin's head

captive   held in a zoo, aquarium, or laboratory instead of living in the wild

clan   large group of orcas made up of several pods

dialect   pattern and style of sounds of a language in a particular place

dolphin   sea mammal related to the whale, but much smaller. Dolphins are 6 to 12 feet (2 to 4 meters) long.

dorsal fin   upright fin on the back of a whale, dolphin, or fish

echolocation   system of finding prey and avoiding obstacles by using sounds and echoes

endangered   in danger of dying out

hydrophone   microphone for detecting sounds under the water

fluke   part of a dolphin's tail

ice floe   flat section of floating ice

instinct   ability that is built into an animal and comes naturally to it

mammal   type of warm-blooded animal that has a backbone, feeds on its mother's milk when young, and has hair on its body

matriline   small group of orcas led by a mother orca

melon   round organ in an orca's forehead, used for beaming out sounds

pod   group of up to 50 orcas, made up of several matrilines

predator   animal that hunts and eats other animals

prey   animal that is eaten by other animals

species   particular type of living thing

streamlined   has a smooth shape that makes it easy to move forward

water pressure   underwater squeezing force caused by the weight of water above

Find Out More

Books

Davidson, Susanna. *Whales and Dolphins* (Usborne Discovery). Tulsa, Okla.: EDC, 2003.

Thomas, Isabel. *Shark vs. Killer Whale* (Animals Head to Head). Chicago: Raintree, 2006.

Throp, Claire. *Orcas* (Living in the Wild: Sea Mammals). Chicago: Heinemann Library, 2013.

Web sites

kids.nationalgeographic.com/kids/animals/creaturefeature/orca
National Geographic has lots of information about orcas, along with a video, e-card, and printout.

www.kidsplanet.org/factsheets/orca.html
Kids' Planet provides useful orca facts.

Places to visit

Orcas Island
www.orcasisland.org
Though it is not actually named after the orca, Orcas Island, off the coast of Washington state, is a great place to spot orcas. There are many whale-watching boat trips and tours available.

SeaWorld
www.seaworld.com
SeaWorld is known for its shows featuring orcas. You can visit SeaWorld parks in San Diego, California; Orlando, Florida; and San Antonio, Texas.

Index

DATE DUE